A Winter Date in Rochester's Park Ave & East Neighborhoods

DATES IN THE STATES

A COUPLE TRAVELING THE UNITED STATES ON A BUDGET

I0459339

Mystery Date
Rochester, NY

By Dates in the States

"Our passion is travel, and we want to share our adventures to inspire others to explore the world with their loved ones. Dare to live beyond the box."

Dates in the States

Introduction

Hey there! We're Crystal and Shane, the duo behind Dates in the States, where we share our love for discovering unique adventures, unforgettable moments, and hidden gems across the U.S. Whether you're searching for a fun date idea, a new place to explore, or just a little inspiration, we've got you covered!

Our Mystery Date Books are designed to help couples (and adventurous friends!) shake up their routine and experience the best local spots in a fun, intentional way. Inside, you'll find a curated collection of date ideas. Each one meant to be completed over the course of a single day in a specific neighborhood. All of which are a surprise until you flip the page!

It's like a little challenge to break out of your comfort zone, support local, and make memories that stick. We hope this book helps you laugh more, explore more, and connect more, with each other and with your city. Let the mystery begin!

Here's What To Expect:

In this City Date Book, we're inviting you on a cozy cold-weather adventure through Rochester, NY, filled with warm sips, lush greenery, unexpected discoveries, and comfort-food favorites.

Here's what to expect for your day ahead:

Begin your date with a soothing cup of tea, setting the tone for a relaxed and unrushed afternoon. From there, step into a tropical plant paradise that feels like a mini escape from the winter chill. Next, explore one of Rochester's most unique museums, a true hidden gem you won't find anywhere else. Wrap up your day with our favorite cider and burgers!

This date is all about slowing down, discovering local gems, and embracing the charm of Rochester, one cozy moment at a time.

Start

Mad Hatter Bakery & Restaurant

229 Alexander Street,
Rochester, NY 14620

Step into the whimsical world of Mad Hatter Bakery and Restaurant, where culinary creativity meets delightful charm. This unique spot offers a delightful array of freshly baked goods, including pastries, cakes, and bread, alongside a menu of savory dishes that are both comforting and innovative. Enjoy a cozy meal or indulge in a sweet treat as you soak in the enchanting atmosphere. Whether you're here for a hearty brunch or a delectable dessert, Mad Hatter promises a memorable dining experience that will tickle your taste buds and delight your senses.

2nd Stop

Lamberton Conservatory

1000 East Avenue,
Rochester, NY 14607

Escape from the cold to discover a tranquil escape at Lamberton Conservatory, a beautiful oasis nestled within Rochester's Highland Park. Explore a stunning collection of exotic plants, vibrant flowers, and lush greenery housed in this charming historical conservatory. Wander through themed gardens and take in the serene atmosphere as you immerse yourself in nature's splendor. Whether you're seeking a peaceful stroll or a picturesque spot for reflection, Lamberton Conservatory offers a refreshing retreat from the everyday.

Third Stop

Artisan Works

565 Blossom Road,
Rochester, NY 14610

Continue your adventure at Artisan Works, an eclectic gallery and creative space that showcases the work of local artists and craftspeople. Wander through an ever-changing collection of art, from paintings and sculptures to mixed media and interactive installations. This vibrant venue offers a unique blend of creativity and community, making it an ideal place to explore and be inspired. Enjoy the diverse exhibits and perhaps even take part in one of their engaging workshops or events, immersing yourself in Rochester's dynamic arts scene.

Fourth Stop

Mullers Cider House

1344 University Ave #180
Rochester, NY 14607

Want to keep going? Simmer down with a drink.
Hungry? Skip this stop and go straight to the end!

Specializing in craft hard ciders from around the world, Muller's offers one of the largest selections in the region, with rotating taps and an extensive bottle list. The laid-back atmosphere makes it an ideal spot to wind down your evening while trying something new, whether you prefer a dry, sweet, or spiced winter cider.

Final Stop

Moo'd Burger Bar

1344 University Ave Ste 110,
Rochester, NY 14607

Sink your teeth into a deliciously unique burger experience at Moo'd Burger Bar. This casual eatery is known for its creative and mouthwatering burger creations, using high-quality ingredients and a variety of toppings to craft the perfect burger for every palate. Enjoy a relaxed atmosphere while savoring their gourmet burgers, tasty sides, and refreshing beverages. Whether you're in the mood for a classic favorite or a bold new flavor combination, Moo'd Burger Bar delivers a satisfying and flavorful dining experience.

Your Memory

Use this space to record
a favorite moment

....
....
....
....
....
....
....
....
....

Add Your Photos

Keepsakes

Thank you for joining us on this mystery date adventure! We hope you've enjoyed the delightful experiences and memorable moments we've crafted just for you in Rochester, NY.

But the adventure doesn't stop here! Keep exploring exciting mystery dates in other cities and uncover new romantic experiences across the U.S. by visiting our website, DatesInTheStates.com. There, you can purchase both physical copies and digital downloads of our mystery date books. Plus, don't miss out on our Mystery Date Book Club, where you can receive a brand-new mystery date book every month!

Tag us in your date photos on social media! @datesinthestates

About the Creators

Crystal, the writer and creator, is a storyteller at heart. When she's not uncovering hidden gems for the next date night idea, she runs her own digital marketing company, helping small businesses improve their content marketing, increase visibility in their communities, and streamline their online presence.
Visit: crystalstatskey.com

Shane, her husband and partner in adventure, is a dedicated personal trainer and the owner of Beekstar Fitness in Irondequoit, NY. He specializes in working with clients who have limited mobility, helping them build muscle and focus on pain areas so they can regain strength and confidence in their daily lives.
Visit: beekstarfitness.com

Crystal and Shane have explored every U.S. state except Alaska (coming soon!) and are now visiting countries in alphabetical order. Whether road-tripping or curating Mystery Date experiences, they'r always chasing their next adventure.

Local Love

A few local gems in Rochester
worth exploring on your next date.

THE DISTILLERY RESTAURANT MT. HOPE

SPORTS BAR & GRILL

1142 MT HOPE AVE, ROCHESTER, NY 14620

EQUAL GROUNDS COMMUNITY CAFE

COZY COFFEESHOP

750 SOUTH AVE, ROCHESTER, NY 14620

HIGHLAND PARK DINER

40'S ERA BOXCAR DINER

960 S CLINTON AVE, ROCHESTER, NY 14620

Want to see your business here?
See the next page for details on
how to join!

Want to be featured?

MYSTERY DATE BOOK PACKAGES

Are you a small business looking to reach new customers? Feature your business in our next Mystery Date Book! Choose from our partnership packages below to connect with couples seeking unique experiences and exclusive deals.

Package One
LOCAL LOVE LISTING

A quick shoutout to show you're part of the neighborhood vibe.

Listed in the "Local Love" section of your designated neighborhood date book

Includes business name, address, and social link

Optional: Offer a small promo (e.g., 10% off for book holders)

1 social media shout-out when the book launches

Package Two
FEATURE STOP

You're not just a business— you're part of the experience.

Marked as a "Must-Stop" on a Mystery Date

Full-page feature in the book with your story, offerings and photo

Includes 1 social media feature — a dedicated post and story highlighting your business

Note: To ensure each feature is genuine and experience-based, we require a hosted visit prior to inclusion.

Package Three
PARTNER & SELLER

Be the spot and the source.

Everything in Tier 2

PLUS: Option to sell the Mystery Date Books at your location

Includes a bulk purchase of 10 books (yours to price + sell)

Keep 100% of the profits from in-store sales

Bonus: Have a featured "sponsored by" page and listed as an official pickup location in our promotions

Prices are subject to change.

Feel free to reach us at any time by sending us an email to say hi and to learn more! We look forward to hearing from you.

| www.datesinthestates.com | datesinthestatesblog@gmail.com |

Sponsors & Affiliates

Our sponsors and affiliates help make our adventures possible! Explore the amazing brands and businesses that support our community.

Wanderful

Wanderful is a global community for women who love to travel. Connect, explore, and join a local hub near you!

Join our Book Club!

Join our Mystery Date Book Club and be part of a travel-inspired community, discovering unique local adventures together!

HomeExchange

HomeExchange lets you swap homes with travelers worldwide for authentic, affordable stays. Join today and travel differently!

Shop our books at a store near you!

Little Button Craft
658 South Ave.
Rochester, NY 14620

The Pawsitive Cat Cafe
120 East Ave. Ste 100
Rochester, NY 14604

Yesterday's Muse Books
32 West Main St.
Webster, NY 14580

Nashville Souvenirs
2613 McGavock Pk,
Nashville, TN 37214

Music Valley Antiques
116 Music Valley Dr.
Nashville, TN 37214

Barnes & Noble
1 Walden Galleria g113,
Buffalo, NY 14225

Abundance Food Co-op
571 South Ave,
Rochester, NY 14620

Union Tavern
4565 Culver Rd,
Irondequoit, NY 14622

DATES IN THE STATES

A COUPLE TRAVELING THE UNITED
STATES ON A BUDGET

Contact Us

🌐

datesinthestates.com

✉

datesinthestatesblog@gmail.com

📍

Based in Rochester, NY

CONNECT WITH US ON SOCIAL!

@DATESINTHESTATES

www.ingramcontent.com/pod-product-compliance
Lightning Source LLC
Chambersburg PA
CBHW041622120626
46551CB00003B/549